Money

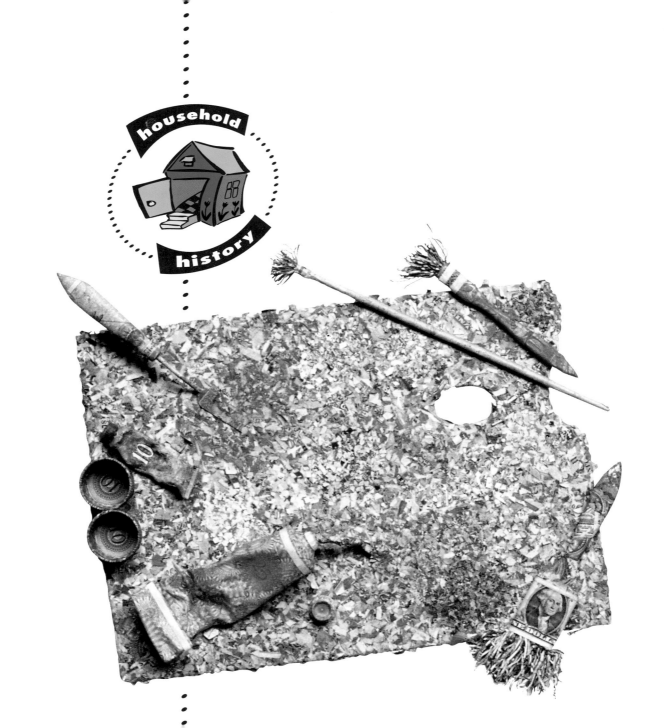

household

history

Money

Robert Young

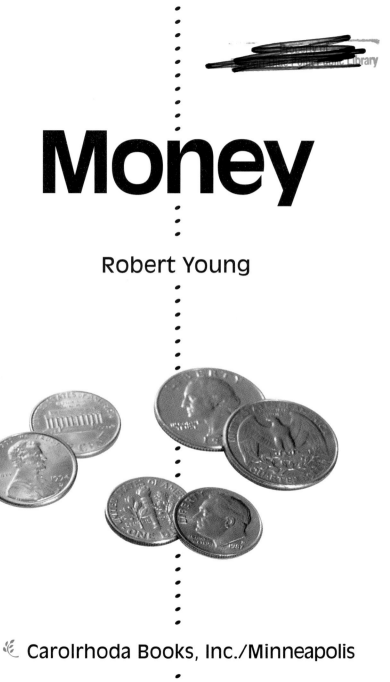

 Carolrhoda Books, Inc./Minneapolis

The photographs in this book are reproduced through the courtesy of: ©Z. Radovan, Jerusalem, cover (upper left); IPS, cover (upper right, lower right, and middle left), pp. 3, 7 (top), 11, 12, 31, 33, 35, 47; Dick Hemingway, cover (middle right), pp. 7 (bottom), 36, 37; American Numismatic Society, cover (bottom middle), pp. 16 (right), 19 (top), 21 (top); ©Richard B. Levine, cover (bottom near left); James Marrinan, cover (bottom far left), pp. 26 (top), 28; Department of the Treasury/ Bureau of Engraving and Printing, p. 1; Barton Lidice Beneš, Mixed Media with Currency, pp. 2, 40; Cheryl Koenig Morgan, p. 5; National Archives, pp. 6 (#121-BA-358B), 29 (#121-BA-361B); John Erste, pp. 8–9, 42–45; Archive Photos/Lambert, #LS143056, p. 10; Norwest Corporation, p. 13; William E. Daehn, pp. 14 (left), 19 (bottom), 20 (both); Museum of the American Numismatic Association, p. 14 (right); National Archives of Canada Neg. No. C1026, p. 15 (top); U.S. Department of Agriculture, p. 15 (bottom); ©William H. Allen, jr., p. 16 (left); Royal Ontario Museum, Toronto, p. 17 (top); ©British Museum, pp. 17 (bottom), 18, 24; Cambridge University Library, p. 22 (top); Erich Lessing/Art Resource, NY, p. 22 (bottom); The Metropolitan Museum of Art, p. 23; Smithsonian Institution, National Numismatic Collection, pp. 21 (bottom), 25 (top), 26 (bottom), 38; Chase Money Museum, p. 25 (bottom); Library of Congress, p. 27; Federal Reserve Bank of Minneapolis, p. 30 (both); Reuters/Michael Urban/Archive Photos #89037001, p. 34; Hollywood Book & Poster, p. 39; Corbis, p. 41; The United States Mint at Denver, p. 46.

For Becky and Boyd, experts at dollars and sense

The author wishes to thank the following people for their generous assistance: Patricia Boerger, Dale Bradley, Dean Hansen, George Hunter, Michael Jones, Debbie Pierce, Virginia Stafford, Kavitha Sundaresan, Ruth Susswein, Gwenyth Swain, Brad Willett, Toni Willett, Sara Young, and Tyler Young. The publisher wishes to thank Dr. Harlan M. Smith, Department of Economics, University of Minnesota.

Words that appear in **bold** in the text are listed in the glossary on page 46.

Carolrhoda Books, Inc. c/o The Lerner Publishing Group
241 First Avenue North, Minneapolis, MN 55401 U.S.A.
Website address: www.lernerbooks.com

Library of Congress Cataloging-in-Publication Data

Young, Robert, 1951–
    Money / Robert Young
        p.   cm. — (Household history)
    Includes index.
    Summary: Surveys the history, development, manufacture, and use of money in its various forms throughout the world.
    ISBN 1-57505-070-6
    1. Money—Juvenile literature. [1. Money] I. Title. II. Series.
HG221.5.Y68 1998
332.4—dc21   97-5287

Manufactured in the United States of America
1 2 3 4 5 6 – JR – 03 02 01 00 99 98

Contents

Money, Money, Money! / 6

All Kinds of Money / 14

Modern Money / 24

We Love Money! / 36

Money Magic / 42

Glossary / 46

Index / 48

Some people like money so much, they find ways to work with it (above) or save it (opposite page, bottom).

Money, Money, Money!

Money. We spend it. We save it. We carry it around in our pockets. Many people collect it. Some people put it on display. Other people wear it. And then there are those who would do anything to get more of it. Those people often end up in jail.

Look around your house. It won't take long before you find some money. Maybe it's a nickel or a dime. Maybe it's a dollar bill, or even more. Money is not hard to find. It's everywhere.

How much money is there? Plenty! In the United States, there are about $3.5 trillion. Just how much is that? Consider this: If you spent a million dollars every day of the year, it would take you more than nine thousand years to spend $3.5 trillion!

Dollars and Cents

Some of that money is in coins. People use about $23 billion worth of coins in the United States. Five different types of coins are made: pennies, nickels, dimes, quarters, and half-dollars.

Some coins have not been popular with the public. In 1979 a new dollar coin was minted. It was named after Susan B. Anthony, who is famous for helping women get the right to vote.

The problem with the coin was its confusing size. The coin was smaller than a half-dollar and only a little bigger than a quarter. The mint stopped making Susan B. Anthony dollars in 1981.

Coins are made by the United States Mint, which has its headquarters in Washington, D.C. The coins we use are made in two branches of the mint, in Denver and Philadelphia. Here's how our coins are made:

The mint buys strips of metal from private companies. For pennies, these strips are made of zinc. (The zinc is coated with copper during the minting process.) For nickels, the strips are a mixture, or **alloy,** of copper and nickel. Dimes, quarters, and half-dollars are made in layers. The outer layers are the same alloy used for nickels. The inner layer is made of copper. The strips of metal are 13 inches wide and 1,500 feet long and weigh about 7,000 pounds each.

At the mints, the metal strips are fed into **blanking machines** that cut out round blanks called **planchets.** These planchets are heated to 1,400 degrees Fahrenheit to soften the metals so they will be easier to stamp. The blanks are cleaned in a chemical bath and then dried.

An **upsetting mill** makes raised rims around the edges of the blanks. The raised rims make the blanks easier to stamp and will help the coins last longer.

Using thousands of pounds of pressure, coining presses stamp the blanks. Coins minted in Denver have a *D* near the date. Other coins, minted at the Philadelphia branch, have a *P* near the date or nothing at all.

As a final step in the minting process, coins are inspected, counted, weighed, and bagged.

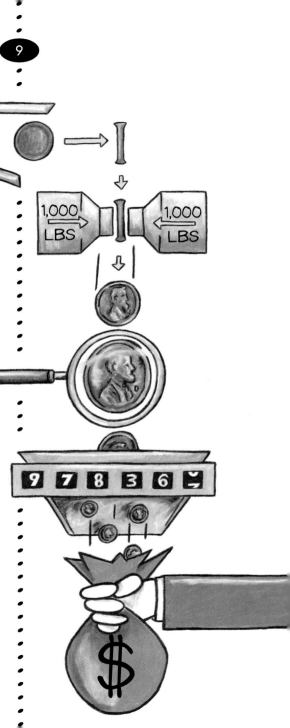

Coins make their way from the upsetting mill (top) into bags and then to a bank near you.

Bills are often called paper money, but they aren't made from trees as most paper is. Bills are made of cotton and linen fibers. More than 35 million bills are printed each day by the United States Bureau of Engraving and Printing in Washington, D.C., and in Fort Worth, Texas. If you stacked those bills on top of each other, the pile would be nearly two miles high!

Every coin has the words *liberty* and *in God we trust* on the front. On the back of every coin, you will find the words *United States of America* and *e pluribus unum,* which is a Latin phrase meaning "out of many, one." This phrase is a reminder. It reminds people to cooperate for the good of the country. It also reminds us how our country began. The United States was formed from many different groups of people, all working to make one nation.

Some of our money is paper money, called bills or notes. There are more than $400 billion in United States paper money. Seven different bills are made for our daily use: the $1, $2, $5, $10, $20, $50, and $100 bills.

A piggy bank rides on top of a pile of play money bills.

Although the values are different, the sizes of the bills are not. Each bill measures 6.14 inches long and 2.61 inches wide, is .0043 inches thick, and weighs .03 troy ounce. (The troy weight system is the most accurate.) Bills are printed in black on the front and in green on the back. No matter what its face value, each bill costs about four cents to make.

Catching Copycats

The government tries to make it hard to **counterfeit,** or copy, bills. The $100 bill has been the most counterfeited bill of all. Here is what the government does to make the $100 bill difficult to copy:

The large portrait of Benjamin Franklin is made of tiny lines, dots, and dashes that are hard to duplicate. A **watermark** portrait of Franklin can be seen from both sides when the bill is held up to a light.

Benjamin Franklin's portrait on the $100 bill sits on a background of dots and dashes that is difficult to copy.

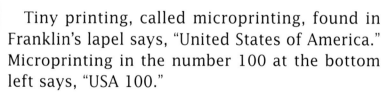

The $100 bill has many features designed to stop counterfeiters.

Technology has made counterfeiting easier. Color copiers and color printers can produce bills that look very much like real money. It may be easy, but is it worth the risk? The punishment for counterfeiting can be as harsh as a five thousand dollar fine and 15 years in prison for each bill you print!

Tiny printing, called microprinting, found in Franklin's lapel says, "United States of America." Microprinting in the number 100 at the bottom left says, "USA 100."

The number 100 at the lower right is printed with color-shifting ink. This ink looks green when you view it straight on but shifts to black when you hold the bill at an angle.

A tiny thread made of polyester runs from top to bottom of each bill. Microprinting in the thread says, "USA 100." The thread can be seen when held up to a light. It glows red when held under an ultraviolet light.

Most money isn't in the form of coins or bills. It's information held in computers at businesses and banks.

Money You Can't Touch

Coins and bills are very common in our lives. But they are not the only kind of money in use. In fact, they are not even the most common type of money. Most money cannot be put into your pocket, or even touched.

This money is in the form of information. The information is held in computers used by banks and businesses. Some of this money will be changed into bills and coins, but most will be transferred to another computer as payment. This is called checkbook money or electronic money. Some people think this money will re- place bills and coins in the future.

Imagine a world without any kind of money. That's the way things began. Thousands of years ago, there was no such thing as money.

All Kinds of Money

Through the ages, money has come in all shapes and sizes, from a boar's tusk (above) to cowrie shells (above, right).

Live without money? How could you do it? It would be very hard today, but it wasn't thousands of years ago. The earliest humans had simple needs: food, clothing, and shelter. Small family groups could take care of these needs themselves.

But in time, as the number of people increased, so did the need for food and other goods. Family groups often traveled together to find things to eat. On their travels, they met other families.

These groups began to trade with each other. This made it easier for people to get the things they wanted.

Let's Make a Deal!

When people began to farm, they grew more food than they needed. They traded the extra food for goods and services from people who had other kinds of jobs, like making clothing, making tools, and protecting the community. This type of trade is called **barter.**

Bartering is still used when people want to make a trade or a payment without using money. But barter doesn't always work. It is often hard to make a fair trade using things that are different. How much corn is a knife worth? What if you have something to trade that nobody wants?

The simple answer is to use money. Money is anything that has value, can be saved, and that people agree to trade with.

Early money was often something people found useful. The early Greeks used oxen for money. People from Egypt and Crete used sheep. In England, during the times of Robin Hood, taxes were paid in horses.

Above: A European trader barters with Native Americans.
Below: Sheep were once used as money.

People in China once used shovels as money.

Salt is important for many reasons: It is a mineral we need in order to stay healthy. For thousands of years, we've used it to season food. And before refrigerators were invented, salt was used to preserve food.

In the first century A.D., Roman soldiers were paid in salt. Our word *salary* comes from *sal,* which means "salt" in Latin.

Tools were very useful to people, so they were used as money too. Some African people used spearheads and knives as money. The Chinese used shovels. Early European settlers in North America used nails.

Salt has been another important form of money. That's right, the same kind of common salt we use in our saltshakers. But it wasn't always so common. Long ago salt was hard to get. Most of it was underground and had to be dug from deep within the earth.

Some early money was whatever people considered pretty. That's why shells were used as money in many parts of the world. People from China, India, and Africa used the cowrie shell.

Iroquois Indians used pieces of whelk shells and quahog clamshells to make beads called **wampum.** These beads were woven into belts and necklaces and used as money. Colonists used wampum made by Native Americans too. In 1626 Peter Minuit, governor of New Netherland, used shells to help buy Manhattan Island. He paid Indians about $25 worth of shells, beads, and knives. Some people believe that this was the best buy in the history of real estate.

Some money was neither useful nor pretty. As late as the 1900s, people who lived on the Pacific islands of Yap used stones for their money. These weren't just any stones. The money was made from aragonite, a brownish white stone with large crystals like quartz. Since there was no aragonite on Yap, people paddled canoes hundreds of miles to another island, Palau, to get the stones. The Yapese worked the stones into round shapes and drilled holes in the middle of them. Then they put sturdy sticks through the holes so that more than one person could help carry the stones. Some of the stones were as big as 12 feet across and weighed more than a ton!

Above: Native American wampum
Below: Traditional Yapese money

People have used many other things as money over the years. Soap, cocoa beans, and elephant-tail hairs have been used. Grain, animal skins, fishhooks, and feathers have also been used. So have tea, tobacco, bird claws, and bear teeth.

Problems with Money

Why aren't these things used for money anymore? Why don't we carry bird claws or salt or shells to the store with us when we want to buy something? The reason is that there were problems with most types of money.

Some money, like grain and beans, spoiled. Other money, like shells and tools and feathers, got smashed or broken. Big rocks and oxen were too big to carry around. Salt was ruined easily. How do you make change when you use sheep or horses for money? And what happens when your money dies?

Money made from metal was different. It didn't spoil, ruin, or break easily. It couldn't die. And it was easy to use. That's why people have been using metal money for almost five thousand years.

At first people used any size or shape of metal. Since precious metals were used, the weight was important. The heavier the piece, the more it was worth. That meant that the pieces of metal had to be weighed. Imagine having your money weighed anytime you wanted to buy something!

Weighing money was a lot of trouble. So some people began marking the metal to show its weight. By marking the metal, they were **minting,** or producing, the first coins. But there was a problem. People did not all weigh and mark the metal the same way. Some people had bad equipment; others were dishonest.

There were other problems with making coins out of valuable metals like gold and silver. When a person needed change, very small coins had to be made. Some ancient coins are so tiny you could put them through an eyelet of your shoe!

This early Roman coin is decorated with tongs and cutters—tools used at a mint.

Opposite page: Kissi pennies are a form of money once used in Africa.
Left: In order to make change, people in ancient times created some very small coins.

Money minted in Lydia is the oldest known currency.

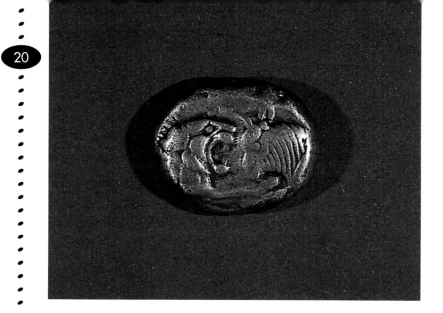

An ancient Greek coin

The First Coins, Bills, & Credit

Around 700 B.C. in Lydia, a small country in what is now Turkey, the king decided that only his men could make coins. Lydia became the first country to make coins. This was the first known **currency,** or money produced by and used in a particular country. Coins from Lydia were different from our coins. They were made of silver and gold. They were oval and looked like small buttons. An emblem, such as a lion's or bull's head, was stamped onto one side.

Around 600 B.C., the Greeks began minting money. They were the first to put designs on both sides of coins. Along with pictures of animals, the Greeks also put the figure of the goddess Athena on coins.

The Romans minted coins beginning around 300 B.C. Their first coins were made of bronze. The largest and heaviest was called an *as.* One hundred of these coins could buy one cow!

Imagine trying to walk around when your pockets are filled with heavy coins. Not very easy, right? Luckily, there is paper money. It makes life easier whenever a lot of money is going to be used.

The Romans made their coins in the temple of Juno Moneta, goddess of marriage and women. From the name *Moneta,* we get our words *mint* and *money.*

The Chinese invented printing in 50 B.C. One hundred and fifty years later, they invented paper. But it wasn't until A.D. 650 that they started printing paper money. Paper money was used more and more often throughout the world as trade between countries grew.

Left: The Chinese were the first to use paper money.

Robbers in Medieval Europe made carrying cash risky.

It wasn't until the 1600s, however, that paper money was used in Europe—and then only thanks to robbers. That's right, robbers! It was not easy to carry lots of coins a long way to buy things. It wasn't safe either, because there were so many robbers. Instead of risking having coins stolen, a person would take them to a goldsmith, a worker who dealt in gold. The goldsmith

Quentin Massys's painting The Money Changer and His Wife *is famous as a detailed portrait of a couple, but it also shows how money was weighed in the 1500s.*

would give the person a receipt. The person could then use the receipt to buy something or to get the coins back.

Sometimes a person would write a note to the goldsmith. The note would direct the goldsmith to pay a certain amount of money to the holder of the note. These notes became the first checks.

There were no credit cards long ago, but there was credit, the system of allowing a person to pay for goods or services at a later date. In Europe during the Middle Ages, knights did not want to carry cash around because of robbers. Instead, knights wore special rings. When a knight stayed at an inn, he stamped the bill with his ring. The innkeeper later took the stamped bill to the knight's castle to be paid.

We don't use special rings to charge things anymore. We don't use notes or receipts from goldsmiths either. And we certainly don't use cocoa beans, fishhooks, or bear teeth to buy things. So how did the money we use come to be?

Knights were the first people to use credit.

Spanish doubloons, also called pieces of eight, were used as money in Colonial America. Coins were cut into pie-shaped pieces, or "bits," to make change.

Modern Money

Imagine you're at a store shopping. When it's time to pay, you reach into your pocket and pull out some coins. But there's a problem: the coins aren't all from the same country. They're from five different countries!

That's what American colonists in the 1600s faced. They had coins from England, France, Spain, Holland, and Portugal. How much was each coin worth? It was very hard to know.

A Pine Tree shilling

In 1652 the Massachusetts Bay Colony decided to do something about the money problem. The colony began making several kinds of silver coins, including the Pine Tree shilling and the Oak Tree shilling. Both were named after pictures on the backs of the coins. England wanted to be in control of the colonies, so it banned the colonists from making coins. But that didn't stop the Massachusetts Bay Colony. The colonists kept making coins for 30 years. How did they keep from getting caught? Simple. They dated all the coins 1652, before the ban.

By the late 1600s, the idea of paper money had spread to North America. But paper money had its problems too. Colonies, banks, counties, cities, and even individuals began printing their own paper money! This became as confusing as trying to use coins from different countries.

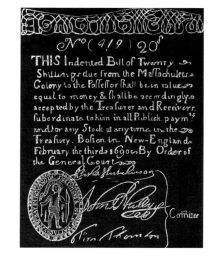

Paper money in Colonial times didn't look much like modern bills.

During the Revolutionary War, Americans used bills called continentals.

The United States of America issued its first coins in 1787.

From Continentals to Greenbacks

In 1775 the colonists were fighting the Revolutionary War against England. To help pay for the war, the Continental Congress decided to print its own money. As the costs of the war increased, the Congress printed more bills than it could redeem from its supply of gold. The Congress printed so many bills, called **continentals,** that the bills were soon worth very little. "Not worth a continental" became a common saying. It meant that something was useless.

For the next 80 years, the government stopped printing paper money. But it did not stop making coins. In 1787, after the United States won its independence, the first national coins were made. They were one-cent pieces made of copper. On them were the words *we are one.*

Still, the new nation had no money system. Finally, in 1792, Congress agreed to make the dollar our basic unit of money. In the same year, Congress also established the first mint in Philadelphia. The first coins made were half-dimes and dimes (spelled d-i-s-m-e-s at the time but said the same way we say it). The silver for the first coins is said to have come from silver tableware donated by George Washington.

During the Civil War, the North and the South needed money to buy supplies and to pay their troops. Both sides began to make their own paper money. The South issued Confederate notes, while the North issued **greenbacks,** named for the green ink used on the backs of the bills.

This bill from 1862 was printed in black on the front and in green on the back, hence the nickname "greenback."

Shinplasters were small in size and worth very little.

Opposite page: Women work to trim the edges of dollar bills in 1907.

The North printed small bills in values of 3, 5, 10, 15, 25, and 50 cents. These bills were worth so little that soldiers used them to line their shoes and to wrap around their shins to keep warm. Soldiers gave these small bills the name **shinplasters.**

The Buck Stops Here

After the war, paper currency was more stable and reliable, but it still didn't look much like the dollar bills we use now. There were a variety of bills called legal tender notes, gold certificates, silver certificates, and national bank notes.

Banks in different states were given a charter, or approval, by the United States government to issue currency. The government guaranteed its paper money. That meant you could take your paper money to a bank and trade it for an equal amount of gold or silver.

But there were problems with having different banks across the country issuing paper money. It was hard to make sure that each bank had enough money on hand to cover withdrawals. And it was difficult for the government to make sure that there were enough bills in the money supply to meet people's needs.

In 1913 the Federal Reserve System was established. The Federal Reserve System issues paper money and oversees the nation's banks. If you look closely at a modern dollar, you'll see that it's called a Federal Reserve Note. It's no longer backed by gold or silver, but we use it because we know people will let us pay for things with it. We also trust that our government will not make big changes in the value of the money. A stable currency makes it easier for people to buy goods and do business.

How can you get your portrait on a United States bill? It helps if you were a founder of this nation or a president. But you don't have to be a household name to get into circulation. Salmon P. Chase worked to end slavery and later set up our nation's banking system. President Abraham Lincoln appointed Chase chief justice of the United States Supreme Court in 1864. His portrait appeared on the $10,000 bill, which was in circulation until the 1960s.

These older bills have been removed from circulation.

When bills are too old to use, many are recycled.

With all the use it gets, most money eventually wears out. The dollar bill has the shortest life. It lasts only about 18 months. During that time, it changes hands about four hundred times, or an average of once every 22 days. Because they aren't used as much, most other bills last longer. On average, $5 bills last about 15 months, $10 bills last 18 months, $20 bills last 2 years, $50 bills last 5 years, and $100 bills last 8 and a half years. Coins are used for about 15 years.

Worn coins are melted down and used to make new coins. Worn bills are shredded. Some shredded bills are recycled and made into roof shingles or fireplace logs. Talk about having "money to burn!"

Abraham Lincoln was the first American to be pictured on a coin. This took place in 1909, the one hundredth anniversary of his birth. The designer of Lincoln's portrait was Victor David Brenner. Look at a penny with a magnifying glass. Can you see the designer's initials, VDB, at the base of the portrait, on Lincoln's right arm? Here are some other things to look for and know about coins:

COIN	PICTURE	DESIGNER	DATE	INITIALS
penny				
(back)	Lincoln Memorial	Frank Gasparro	1959	bottom right
nickel				
(front)	Thomas Jefferson	Felix Schlag	1938	below portrait
(back)	Monticello, Jefferson's home			
dime				
(front)	Franklin Roosevelt	John R. Sinnock	1946	below neck
(back)	flaming torch, olive and oak branches			
quarter				
(front)	George Washington	John Flanagan	1932	lower neck
(back)	eagle standing on arrows and olive branch			
half-dollar				
(front)	John F. Kennedy	Gilroy Roberts	1964	lower neck
(back)	presidential coat of arms	Frank Gasparro	1964	below eagle

Here's how a check works:

1. Person A writes a check to person B.
2. Person B takes the check to a bank. After signing, or endorsing, the back of the check, person B cashes it.
3. The bank sends the cancelled check back to person A's bank.
4. The amount of the check is subtracted from person A's account.

When do you think it's better to write a check rather than pay in cash?

Checking Things Out

Checks were first used in Colonial America in 1681. They were used because there weren't enough coins and bills to go around. A group of businessmen put their gold and silver together and started to write checks.

A check is a written order to a bank to pay the person receiving the check from money that is on deposit at the bank. Many people would not accept the first checks. They did not trust the checks' value.

A hundred years later, cities had grown, transportation had improved, the postal system was dependable, and people were putting their money in banks. Checks became a safe and easy way to pay for things. It was easier to send a check than it was to send cash in the mail. It was also safer to carry a checkbook than piles of bills that could be lost or stolen.

By the time of the Civil War, checks had become popular. And that was just the start of things. More than 85 percent of American families have a checking account. Americans write more than 60 billion checks each year. That comes to about 260 million checks every business day. If those checks were put end to end, they would stretch for about 20 thousand miles. That's long enough to reach across the United States six times. In fewer than 2 days there would be enough checks to circle the earth. It would only take about 12 days' worth of checks to reach the moon!

Paying with Plastic

The credit card is another safe and easy way to pay. Credit, the system of allowing people to pay later, has been around for a long time. But credit cards didn't appear in the United States until the early 1900s. Hotels were the first to offer cards to their customers. Customers used the plastic cards to pay for their hotel stays and were billed at the end of the month. By the 1920s, department stores and gas companies offered cards too. All these cards, however, could only be used at the business that issued them.

That began to change with the start of Diners Club cards in 1950. These cards could be used at many different restaurants and hotels. Then, in 1951, some banks began issuing credit cards. These could be used at restaurants, hotels, and many more places. In the following years, other credit cards appeared.

Credit cards are especially handy when it comes to buying things over the telephone.

Have you ever heard of a credit card collector? Walter Cavanagh of California is known as "Mr. Plastic Fantastic." He has more than 1,300 credit cards, the largest collection in the world. He keeps his cards in the world's longest wallet. It is 250 feet long!

Are credit cards popular? Just think about this: There are more than one billion credit cards being used in the world. The average adult in the United States has between 8 and 10 credit cards. In one year, cards are used to buy more than $500 billion worth of goods and services!

Credit cards are convenient—sometimes too convenient. They allow people to buy things quickly and easily, with the understanding that they will pay later. People must make sure they can pay for the things they charge. Otherwise, they may end up owing a lot of money.

Computers have changed the way we use money and the kinds of money we use. Less than 1 out of every 10 dollars in the United States money supply is in the form of coins and bills. The rest is checkbook money and electronic money. Computers help people make all kinds of payments. Automated Teller Machines (ATMs) help people make deposits, transfers, or get cash when banks are closed or not nearby.

A stored-value card, also called an "electronic purse," has a tiny computer chip in it. The chip stores a certain amount of money value. A person can use the card to buy things from businesses with machines that accept the card. When the card's money value has been used up, the card can be reloaded at ATMs, special terminals, or over the telephone. A stored-value card can take the place of coins and bills.

From shells and fishhooks to plastic and computer chips, money has come a long way over the years. It has become a very important part of our lives. If you want to know just how important money is, take a look around you.

Automated Teller Machines (ATMs) help make banking more convenient.

Money is so much a part of our culture, we even play with it.

We Love Money!

What do you see that does not cost money? Not much. The fact is, we have to have money for the same simple needs people have had through time: food, clothes, and shelter. Money also helps us go places and have fun. It gives us choices.

Money is important for kids as well as for adults. That's why there are books to help children earn, save, and even invest their money. Money skills are taught in schools. Many banks offer programs for kids. There is even a bank just for children and young adults!

The Young Americans Bank opened in Denver, Colorado, in 1987. Only people 21 years of age or younger can bank there. They can open checking and savings accounts. They can also apply for loans and credit cards. More than 17 thousand kids do their banking at the Young Americans Bank. It has customers from all 50 states and from 10 foreign countries.

Collectible Coins

Spending and saving are not the only things people do with money. Millions of people collect it. The study or collection of money is called **numismatics.** This term comes from the Greek word *nomisma,* which means "coin in circulation."

Millions of people collect money.

More people collect money than anything else except stamps. Some collect paper money, but most collect coins. The United States Mint in San Francisco produces sets of **proof coins** for collectors. These coins are made in such a way that they have very few imperfections. Then they are sealed in plastic. They have not been circulated, or used.

The mint also sells **uncirculated coins** and **commemorative coins.** Uncirculated coins are regular coins that have not been used. Commemorative coins are special coins that honor famous people or events.

Commemorative coins honor important people in history, such as Booker T. Washington.

Money Talk

Money is important to more than just collectors. Why else would people write about it, sing about it, and make movies about it? There are even sayings about money. Do you know what the following expressions mean? Do you think they are true?

"Money can't buy happiness."
"Money talks."
"The love of money is the root of all evil."
"Money doesn't grow on trees."
"A fool and his money are soon parted."
"Time is money."

Many songs have been written about money over the years. Ask your parents or grandparents about money songs they have heard. Do they remember "Three Coins in the Fountain?" What about "We're in the Money" or "If I Were a Rich Man"? "Money for Nothing" became a top hit for the rock band Dire Straits in 1985. "Money Don't Matter 2 Night" by the singer then called Prince was a hit song in 1992.

Actor Cuba Gooding Jr. made the phrase "Show me the money!" popular in the movie Jerry Maguire.

Money may not grow on trees, but you can still grow it. *Lunaria annua,* also known as the money plant, starts out as seeds, not pieces of gold or silver. In the spring, beautiful white, lavender, or purple flowers appear. In late summer or fall, seedpods that look like silver dollars grow. Enjoy them. But don't try to spend them!

Artist Barton Beneš finds inspiration in money.

Money You Can't Spend

Money products are all around us, but you can't spend them. You can use money pencils to write on paper that looks like bills. You can tell the time with money watches and wear money jewelry. And, of course, don't forget chocolate coins with gold wrappers. We love to be around money, even if it isn't real!

Money is such an important part of our lives that it is used by many artists in their work. Barton Beneš, an artist from New York City, makes things out of bills and objects. By cutting, folding, and gluing the bills, Beneš transforms ordinary objects and creates works of art.

Another artist uses his art *as money*. Artist J. S. G. Boggs draws pictures of bills. His pictures look so real, he could probably use the bills without telling people they're fake. Instead, Boggs tells people that his artwork has as much value as the bill he is copying. He lets people decide if they want to take his drawings as payment.

Many people do. Over a few years, Boggs was able to "spend" more than 700 of his drawings. The goods and services he got for them were worth more than $35 thousand.

Money will always be an important part of our lives. We will name songs and movies and plants after it. We will earn it and save it and spend it too. But money will not always stay the same. Think of all the changes money has gone through since people first started trading sheep and salt and shells. Imagine what it will be like in the future!

Costume designer Lizzy Gardiner loves the look of money so much, she designed a dress made from credit cards.

Money Magic

Here are some fun things to do with money:

You Will Need:

4 pennies

chewing gum or tape

1. Put three pennies on a table. Tell your friends that you're going to make an extra penny. Push the pennies into your hand and then close it. Say some magic words. Open up your hand and count the pennies. There are now four!

   The trick is to stick an extra penny under the edge of the table. You can do this with a small piece of chewing gum or tape. When you push the pennies on the table into your hand, slide the penny off from underneath.

2. Tell your friends you can make a nickel disappear. Get a clear glass, a dark cloth, and a nickel. Hold the glass in your open palm and show the nickel at the bottom of it. Then cover the glass with the cloth. Say some magic words, then pull off the cloth. The nickel has disappeared.

You Will Need:

clear drinking glass

dark cloth

nickel

The trick is to put the nickel on your palm instead of in the glass. (It will look like it's in the glass.) When you say the magic words, hold the top of the glass with your other hand for a moment while you take the nickel out and slip it into your pocket.

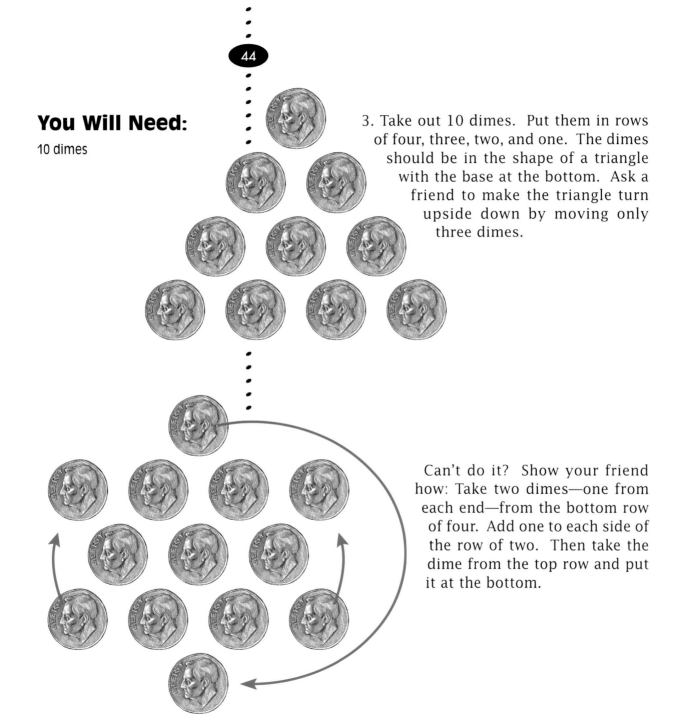

You Will Need:

10 dimes

3. Take out 10 dimes. Put them in rows of four, three, two, and one. The dimes should be in the shape of a triangle with the base at the bottom. Ask a friend to make the triangle turn upside down by moving only three dimes.

Can't do it? Show your friend how: Take two dimes—one from each end—from the bottom row of four. Add one to each side of the row of two. Then take the dime from the top row and put it at the bottom.

4. Find a new $5 bill. Ask your friends if they can find the names of 10 states on the bill. They will look hard, but they probably won't find them.

You Will Need:

a crisp $5 bill

magnifying glass

Now it's your turn. Look on the back of the bill. Along the top of the Lincoln Memorial are the names of the states. They are written very small, a little less than a quarter inch above the top of the pillars. You will need a magnifying glass to see them.

Glossary

alloy: a mixture of metals

barter: to trade goods and services without using money

blanking machines: presses that cut blank coins from strips of metal

commemorative coins: coins made to honor a person or an event

continentals: bills produced by the American colonists during the Revolutionary War

counterfeit: to copy illegally

currency: coins and paper money used in a country

greenbacks: paper money issued by the North during the Civil War. Greenbacks were named for the color of the ink on the back of the bills.

minting: making money by stamping metal. A mint is the place where coins are made.

numismatics: the study or collection of money

planchets: round, blank pieces of metal. When they are stamped, planchets become coins.

proof coins: coins specially made for collectors

shinplasters: small bills of very little value used to line the shoes of Union soldiers during the Civil War

uncirculated coins: coins that have not been used

upsetting mill: a machine that takes blank coins, or planchets, and produces a raised, or upset, rim

wampum: beads made of small shells. Wampum was used as money by some Native Americans and colonists.

watermark: a design formed by varying the density of fibers when making a sheet of paper. A watermark can be seen when the paper is held up to a light.

Index

alloy, 8, 46
Anthony, Susan B., 7
Automatic Teller Machines
   (ATMs), 35

barter, 15, 46
Beneš, Barton, 40
bills, 10–11, 12, 13, 27–28,
   29, 30, 32, 40, 46, 47
blanking machines, 8, 46
Boggs, J. S. G., 41
Brenner, Victor David, 31

Cavanagh, Walter, 34
Chase, Salmon P., 29
checks, 23, 32, 35, 37
China, 16, 21
coins, 7–10, 13, 19–21, 24,
   25, 26, 27, 30, 31, 46, 47.
   See also commemorative
   coins, proof coins, *and*
   uncirculated coins
commemorative coins, 38, 46
continentals, 26, 46
counterfeiting, 11–12, 46
credit, 23, 33
credit cards, 23, 33, 34, 37
currency, 20, 28, 29, 46

Denver, Colo., 8, 9, 37
Diners Club, 33

England, 15, 24, 25, 26

Federal Reserve Note, 29
Federal Reserve System, 29
Fort Worth, Tex., 10
Franklin, Benjamin, 11–12

Greece, Ancient, 15, 20
greenbacks, 27, 47

Lincoln, President Abraham,
   29, 31
Lydia, 20

Manhattan Island, 17
Massachusetts Bay Colony,
   25
microprinting, 12
Mint, the United States, 7,
   8–9, 27, 38
minting, 8–9, 19, 47
Minuit, Peter, 17
money: American, 7–12,
   24–33; and art, 40–41; and
   children, 36–37; collecting,
   6, 34, 37–38, 39, 47; early
   forms, 15–18; electronic,
   13, 35; expressions, 39;
   history, 14–35;
   manufacturing, 8–9, 19,
   20; songs, 39, 41. *See also*
   bills, coins, *and* minting
money magic, 42–45
money plant, 40

Native Americans, 17, 47
New Netherland, 17
numismatics, 37, 47. *See
   also* money collecting

Oak Tree shilling, 25

Philadelphia, Pa., 8, 9, 27
Pine Tree shilling, 25
planchets, 8–9, 47
proof coins, 38, 47

Rome, Ancient, 16, 21

salt, 16, 41
shinplasters, 28, 47
stored-value card, 35

uncirculated coins, 38, 47
United States, 7, 10, 12, 26,
   28, 29, 33, 34, 35
United States Bureau of
   Engraving and Printing, 10
United States Mint, the. *See*
   Mint, the United States
upsetting mill, 9, 47

wampum, 17, 47
War, Civil, 27–28, 32, 47
Washington, D.C., 8, 10
Washington, President
   George, 27
watermark, 11, 47

Yap Islands, 17
Young Americans Bank, 37